Cortège

Cortège

Carl Phillips

[signature]

Graywolf Press
Saint Paul

Publication of this volume is made possible in part by a grant
provided by the Minnesota State Arts Board through an appropriation
by the Minnesota State Legislature, and by a grant from the National
Endowment for the Arts. Significant additional support has been
provided by the Andrew W. Mellon Foundation, the Lila Wallace-
Reader's Digest Fund, the McKnight Foundation, and other generous
contributions from foundation, corporations, and individuals.
Graywolf Press is a member agency of United Arts, Saint Paul.
To these organizations and individuals who make our work possible,
we offer heartfelt thanks.

Published by Graywolf Press
2402 University Avenue, Suite 203
Saint Paul, Minnesota 55114

Printed in the United States of America.

ISBN 1-55597-230-6

9 8 7 6 5 4 3 2
2 4 6 8 9 7 5 3
First Graywolf Printing, 1995

Library of Congress Catalog Card Number 95-077948

Acknowledgments

Grateful acknowledgment is made to the editors of the journals
in which some of the poems herein originally appeared or are forth-
coming: *Agni:* "Cortège," "A Mathematics of Breathing"; *Antioch
Review:* "Somewhere Holy" (as "For Erin, for Others"); *Boston
Phoenix:* "Toys"; *Boston Review:* "A Touring Man Loses His Way";
Callaloo: "The Reach," "Sunday"; *Chelsea:* "Seminar: Problems in
Renaissance Painting," "Teaching Ovid to Sixth-Graders"; *Hawai'i
Review:* "Levitation"; *Indiana Review:* "Domestic," "King of Hearts,"
"The Photographer"; *The Journal:* "The Compass" (as "Processional");
Kenyon Review: "Cotillion," "Glads," "Our Lady"; *Muleteeth:* "In the
Picture"; *The Nebraska Review:* "Freeze"; *The Paris Review:* "The
Swain's Invitation," "Youth with Satyr, Both Resting";
Ploughshares: "What Myth Is"; *Poet Lore:* "Any Moment"; *Poetry
Northwest:* "Lullaby for the Wounded Eros"; *Webster Review:* "Kit,"
"One sees pictures of Dante:" "Pygmalion," "Your Dream";
Witness: "Aubade for Eve Under the Arbor," "I See a Man."

"Toys" also appeared in the anthology *The Best American Poetry 1995,*
edited by Richard Howard and David Lehman, published by Charles
Scribner's Sons in 1995.

"The Mathematics of Breathing" also appeared in *The Best American
Poetry 1994,* edited by A. R. Ammons and David Lehman, published by
Charles Scribner's Sons in 1994; and in *On the Verge: Emerging Poets
and Artists,* edited by Thomas Sayers Ellis and Joseph Lease, published
by Agni Press in 1993.

"Cortège" also appeared in a limited edition feuilleton series produced
by Feuillets, a division of Helicon Nine Editions, and published by
Midwest Center for the Literary Arts, Kansas City, Missouri.

I wish to thank Frank Bidart, Allison Funk, Doug Macomber, Fred
Marchant, Robert Pinsky, and Lloyd Schwartz for their invaluable
assistance with the manuscript and their immeasurable patience
with the author.

For Doug

Contents

The unendurable is the beginning of the curve of joy.

Djuna Barnes, *Nightwood*

Cortège

The Compass

a star

dog with torch in its mouth

a finger-ring   but no finger
broken cup   what is lonely
the single breast the beehive resembles
a pair of breasts on a dish

what else
comes in pairs   tongs   forceps
a key crossing a key
the cross but   recumbent or

knocked over
what is called the cross saltire
t
turned on its side

x
that one and
that one and
what stands for

gridiron for the having been roasted alive
a ship's windlass for around
what the intestine   pulled out into
the salt air   was bound fast

what flies   a raven
a winged lion
a winged ox
a man   but with wings

an arrow

what is lovely   an arrow

I

I See a Man

He has just had sex. I can tell by the way, when he
notices his shadow ahead of him, broad, spilling over both
curbs to the road he is walking down slowly, most of him
wants to stop and, as if remembering, stand briefly at a
kind of attention. He has just had sex, it's unclear with
whom. It was a man, it was a woman . . . it was the air, whose
inconveniently wide-apart edges can be all day coming together.
There's this sense in which it can't matter—sex being,
for him, any attempt to fill a space in so there's no room
left, for a while, for what he surely calls a suffering inside
him—that much his brow gives away, his mouth too, designed,
it seems, for delivering lines like *Already, as far into
the world as I've wanted, I've come.* He's thirty, thirty-two—
it's easy, still, to say a thing like that. Write it down,
even. Call it a poem.

The Swain's Invitation

The barn is warm, come inside, lie down,
sleep. Here, no sheep ever fails

in jumping, tears its dug or anything
else tender on the fencing's barbed wire

and, losing all the grace that true
jumping is made of, leaves you, flushed,

to start all over again counting.
If later on in the night one sheep, over

another, appeals, stirs in you, somewhere,
something, be easy, no gate will fall

closed, forbid you trespass; what you want—
why shouldn't you, why can't you? Take it:

the easy-to-grip flank that has always
worn your mark on it; for pillow,

the woolly side, still trembling,
after; the broad tongue, meat-pink,

for washing a thing back toward clean,
that place where, at last,

there's no trouble in sleeping, or
dreaming, or in remembering, by dawn,

only how tired you were, how warm the barn.

Kit

At first,
the more obvious, slack-chested tokens may
come to mind: the lone and tankless

gasoline pump, the dry gun at last receiving
a good oil. For mood: lamps, but
flickering, in need of a strong circuit,

candles, guttering the way they do, in their
small wells.
Rising is too easy; easier still, the stepping,

as from scum-sheeted water, away: resist it;
lie facedown, spread-eagled, lie smooth as
blades, that quiet. Know that his coming

may not be as you've expected, in the lulling
manner of dragonflies alighting
on whatever it is seems most fragile:

the cosmos-flower, unfolding again for the sun,
the yellow rockets, forever launching from
their stems.

You may find
that taking his unknown quantity upon you will
require imagination on your part: suggestions

include any man mouthing his hands clear of
fried chicken,
a saint drawing fresh from his wounds his thin

fingers, and taking each one to his mouth.
It may not seem
like ecstasy, exactly. It may be something

less, at first, like joy that runs you through.

The Hustler Speaks of Places
(after Langston Hughes)

I've known places:
I've known places weary as the flesh when it's had some,
    as rivers at last done with flowing.

My soul has been changed in places.

I mouthed a man dry in the Ritz-Carlton men's room.
I built a life upon a man's chest and, briefly, found peace.
I watched a man sleeping; I raised a prayer over his brow.
I heard the stinging, in bars, of lashes coming down on a
    man's bare ass, until it tore to the red that is sunset.

I've known places:
shaven, uncut places.

My soul has been changed in places.

King of Hearts

Somewhere now, someone is missing him,
since here he is for the taking, nicked
at three of his four corners, decked out

in the fade of much play, his two heads
laid prone on the sidewalk before you.

Like you, in this heat and humidity, no
wind, when it comes, moves him. Like you,

he knows a thing, maybe, about wilting—
how, like sleep or some particularly

miserable defeat played over but this time
in slow motion, it has its own fine beauty.

     *

Tonight,
         once you've found him, when you've

brought him home, the man with a face as
close as you'll ever get to the other one,

the one it was easy enough, earlier, not to
pick up, to step on, even, and move slowly

but unbothered away from, you'll only remember

the part about wilting.
          And even that, as

you lift his ass toward you, as your hands
spread it open until it resembles nothing

so much as a raw heart but with a seemingly
endless hole through it—even that will

fade.
      Him, between drink and the good money

you've paid, doing whatever you tell him.
Him throwing back whatever words you hand out.

You're the king, you're the king, him saying.

Sunday

I. God

All morning, I watch him.
Good shirt and—showing, but just—white briefs.
Nothing else, really; any man, balconied, smoking.
Rusted barbecue grill at his side for an ashtray.
Cars, parked three floors down, serving too.
Sometimes, wind catches at his shirttails; they rise, slightly.
When the wind goes away, so does the bloom.

II. Ecstasy

Later, after gathering the mint from beneath the one tree,
after plucking each leaf, but fiercely, as if there
must somewhere be something else; after chopping the mint,
boiling the potatoes, after rolling the potatoes in butter,
and then mint, then again butter, I stop to smell
each of my fingers. Something has changed.
Not one of them smells like you did.

III. Heaven

There are fowl, I am sure; each walks free, across nothing.
There are cookbooks, overlong recipes for which there is
finally time, but no hunger. Now and then, tasks, all simple.
Baking, for the hands. Things to stir—rainwater, feathers in
steep barrels—to show patience, what eternity requires.
Elsewhere, on roads that wind to nowhere but cloud,
the changing of tires, reminding how it feels to be stranded.

The Reach

Out here, where any rambling bed—of sea-
moss, pachysandra—serves more times than not
for what, before, elsewhere, I used to call
the real thing, whole days can pass and still

no hurry, just the flesh and, everywhere,
the languorous slow drifting toward the next
good thing to feed it, meaning mainly food,
but also something more—not joy, exactly,

and not quite sex: think of what, once joy,
then sex, has been stripped down, is left behind:
that's it, or close. Here, the only rule
the body still holds true is, at whatever

cost, to know always how to hold itself:
not just the back, though posture, yes, matters
here, but in knowing when to turn the face,
whichever of its sides should more displease,

away from light, the less to give offense;
or how to place the one foot, booted, ankle-
braceleted, so, before the other. Am
I happy? Mostly. Still, this time of year,

the season gone, I wander into clubs,
now close to empty, watch the one or two
stray pairs of men slow dance around and through
the ghosts of those I'll see next summer and all

the rest, who won't return, ever, and some-
thing, passing in and out, through my own
body, stops short, and founders. Certain nights,
lately, I walk down streets the wind alone

bothers to sweep clean now—and missing that
flesh-to-the-flesh abrading I am told
here means desire, the low to lower pitch-
ing of the voice I've come to recognize

as any body when it sings, at last,
at last fed, I try to make a small noise
myself, to sing . . . and can't. It seems I'm still
too new to this; the sea, however close,

is one more untried stranger: everytime I
open my mouth, it fills with salt or what
amounts to salt, it feels just like it, left
sticky and heavy—foreign—on my tongue.

Our Lady

In the final hour, our lady—Of
the electric rosary, Of the highway,
by then Of the snows mostly—was

the man he'd always been really,
though, yes, we'd sometimes forgotten.
Still, even while he lay fanning,

as one might any spent flame, where
it was hot, between his legs, and
saying it didn't much matter anymore

about dying, what came of having
come too often, perhaps, to what in
the end had fallen short of divine

always, he said that more than the
bare-chested dancers and all-conquering
bass-line that had marked his every

sudden, strobe-lit appearance, at
precisely the same moment, in all of
the city's best clubs; more than

the just-heated towels and the water
he'd called holy in those windowless,
too thinly-walled, now all but

abandoned bath-houses, he regretted
the fine gowns that he'd made, just
by wearing them, famous; and then,

half, it seemed, to remind us, half
himself, he recreated the old shrug,
slowly raising from his hospital

robe—not green, he insisted, but
two shades, maybe three, shy of
turquoise—one shoulder to show

the words still tattooed there:
Adore me; for a moment, it was
possible to see it, the once

extraordinary beauty, the heated
grace for which we'd all of us,
once, so eagerly sought him.

Cotillion

Every one of these bodies, those in drag, those
not, loves a party, that much is clear. The blonde
with the amazing lashes–lashes, more amazingly,

his own–tells me it is like when a small bird
rises, sometimes, like the difficult thing is not to.
I think he is talking about joy or pain or desire

or any of the several things desire, sweet drug,
too sweet, can lead to. I think he means moments,
like this one, sudden, when in no time I know that

these lashes, the mouth that could use now more
painting, these hairless, shaven-for-the-event arms
whose skin, against the shine of the gown, a spill of

blood and sequins the arms themselves spill from,
glitters still, but dully, like what is not the
main prize does always–I know this man is mine,

if I want him. Meanwhile around us, the room fairly
staggers with men, and an aching to be lovely, loved,
even. As in any crowd, lately, of people, the heavy

corsage of them stepping in groups, the torn bloom
that is each taking his own particular distance,
I think the trick is one neither of joining or not

joining, but of holding, as long as I can, to some
space between, call it rest for the wary, the slow
dragging to nowhere I call heaven. I'm dancing

maybe, but not on air: this time through water.

II

Cortège

Do not imagine you can abdicate
                                        Auden

Prologue

If the sea could dream, and if the sea
were dreaming now, the dream
would be the usual one: Of the Flesh.
The letter written in the dream would go
something like: *Forgive me—love, Blue.*

I. The Viewing (A Chorus)

O what, then, did he look like?
       He had a good body.

And how came you to know this?
       His body was naked.

Say the sound of his body.
       His body was quiet.

Say again—quiet?
       He was sleeping.

You are sure of this? Sleeping?
       Inside it, yes. Inside it.

II. Pavilion

Sometimes, a breeze: a canvas
flap will rise and, inside,
someone stirs; *a bird? a flower?*

One is thinking *Should there be*
thirst, I have only to reach
for the swollen bag of skin

beside me, I have only to touch
my mouth that is meant for a flower
to it, and drink.

One is for now certain he is
one of those poems that stop only;
they do not end.

One says without actually saying it
I am sometimes a book of such poems,
I am other times a flower and lovely

pressed like so among them, but
always they forget me.
I miss my name.

They are all of them heat-
weary, anxious for evening as for
some beautiful to the bone

messenger to come. They will open
again for him. His hands are good.
His message is a flower.

III. The Tasting (A Chorus)

O what, then, did he taste like?
　　　　　　　　He tasted of sorrow.

And how came you to know this?
　　　　　　　　My tongue still remembers.

Say the taste that is sorrow.
　　　　　　　　Game, fallen unfairly.

And yet, you still tasted?
　　　　　　　　Still, I tasted.

Did you say to him something?
　　　　　　　　I could not speak, for hunger.

IV. Interior

And now,
the candle blooms gorgeously away
from his hand—

and the light has made
blameless all over
the body of him (mystery,

mystery), twelvefold
shining, by grace of twelve
mirrors the moth can't stop

attending. Singly, in no order,
it flutters against, beats
the glass of each one,

as someone elsewhere
is maybe beating upon
a strange door now,

somebody knocks
and knocks at a new
country, of which

nothing is understood—
no danger occurs
to him, though

danger could be any
of the unusually wild
flowers

that, either side of the road,
spring.
When he slows, bends down and

closer, to see or
to take one—it is as if
he knows something to tell it.

V. The Dreaming (A Chorus)

O what, then, did it feel like?
       I dreamed of an arrow.

And how came you to know him?
       I dreamed he was wanting.

Say the dream of him wanting.
       A swan, a wing folding.

Why do you weep now?
       I remember.

Tell what else you remember.
       The swan was mutilated.

Envoi

And I came to where was nothing but drowning
and more drowning, and saw to where the sea—
besides flesh—was, as well, littered with boats,
how each was blue but trimmed with white, to each
a name I didn't know and then, recalling,
did. And ignoring the flesh that, burning, gives
more stink than heat, I dragged what boats I could
to the shore and piled them severally in a tree-
less space, and lit a fire that didn't take
at first—the wood was wet—and then, helped by
the wind, became a blaze so high the sea
itself, along with the bodies in it, seemed
to burn. I watched as each boat fell to flame:
Vincent and *Matthew* and, last, what bore your name.

III

Youth with Satyr, Both Resting

There are certain words—*ecstasy, abandon,*
surrender—we can wait all our lives,
sometimes,

not so much to use,
as to use correctly;
then the moment at last comes,

the right scene but more impossibly
different than any we'd earlier imagined,
and we stumble, catching

instead at nouns like *desire,* that
could as easily be verbs,
unstable adjectives like *rapt* or *unseemly.*

We find that for once nothing at hand
serves quite as well as the finger doing
what it does, pointing:

at the wine whose slim remains
the two glasses—tipped slightly, given
over to the grass as to their own sweet brand

of longing—look like any moment
letting go of;
or the boy's hand, fallen in such a way as

to just miss
touching the predictably stiff phallus—no
other word here will do—of the satyr;

or at how the O of the boy's mouth,
barely open,
is the same O that the satyr's beard, abruptly

arching away from his shag-covered chest, and
on, skyward,
seems most like wanting to curl into, if only

it could . . . which in turn is
the same O repeated by those the grapes'
twisting vines—too artificially, perhaps—

string above and,
to either side of the two sleepers,
in the manner of any number of unresolvable

themes, let dangle.

Glads

Three, at the most four days later,
they're dying, knuckled
over at whichever flower has bloomed

largest. The way everything beautiful
finally breaks because of, from it.
As if this were necessary. The reason,

maybe, why the loveliest things are always
also the most ruined:
a man's aging breast falling until,

naturally, brassieres come to mind;
or why, given any crumbled wall, nobody
thinks to ask where did they go to,

bring them back, all those
missing pieces.
The difference between a cock at plain

rest, for once longing to put itself
nowhere special,
and one that, just done thirsting,

collapses, curls slowly back in on
itself.
In Renaissance Italy,

when depicting the saints and Christ
in mid-torment was all the rage,
the painters chose for their backdrops

the most unremarkable buildings,
landscapes stranded in neutral, people
doing the dull things they still do—

plowing, benchwarming a small hill,
idly swinging a staff at livestock,
or at nothing, gone fishing.

The idea was to throw up into relief,
in its rawest form, sheer affliction.
The motto was

No distractions from suffering, hence
the skies: in general, clear
or just clearing, washed of anything

like rescue birds hope clouds mercy.

Teaching Ovid to Sixth-Graders

Easy enough, now,
listening to this uneven rustle
of sleeved arms over paper,

to imagine what Ganymede heard,
desire, and the new life to be spent
bending

for a body that already had undone
so many,
on wings approaching.

I look at their arms,
things I sometimes have thought
I would not mind learning,

in my own way, to love, and I wonder—
even now, after Ganymede
and all the other names I have told them

for the flesh in defeat—
what do these bodies know, really,
that I wanted them to,

how any myth
is finally about the lengths the mind will
carry a tale to, to explain what the body

knows already, and so never answers:
that there *is* no way to explain
what can happen,

what can take a life
that does not mean harm
just as suddenly and terribly

down, for all that.
Pacing the aisles,
I dream my mouth to each ear,

the lesson beginning
all over again,
but different.

One sees pictures of Dante:

in Byzantine profile, looking about
as visionary as the next unremarkable bird;
frozen in an encounter with Beatrice on a
significant bridge or some tumbledown
strada, about to lose her all over again.
My own picture is more plastic:

the maestro, leaning stiffly out
from the roofless carriage of exile,
has his eye on the hands of a particular
young man just off of the roadside, lifting
the salvageable pieces of fruit
from the ground, and in a bucket he has brought
for the purpose, rinsing each separately
free of dirt, then paring away the soft,
inedible portions.
                              It is another of those
afternoons when he can hardly endure
the ride home, he's that eager
to put it all down, that certain that each
of the man's beautiful gestures must
in some way concern the soul.

Seminar: Problems in Renaissance Painting

In the first panel, for example: the way,
for all his being an angel, it's still his
perfect, not-yet-arrived body one keeps
wondering at most, that and the eyes with
their look that seems, but can't possibly
mean, to say Fuck me;

                            or in the second panel,
on the virgin's otherwise bare table, that
lily open too wide too soon, bending sunward
at an angle nothing living should have to:

surely this was not the artist's intention.

Better to have painted, for the lily, one of
those flowers that opens only at night. Say
it's morning, and the virgin—as much Mary
as any woman, or man, even—

                            is touching
the closed head, the spent-all-over-again
leaves. Noticing only how each stroke feels,
like longing, she hasn't noticed yet

what goes on in the third panel, behind her:
the old life, in the manner of robes loosened,
beginning to fall slightly;

the angel shouldering his way into the room.

Toys

Seeing them like this,
arranged according to size,
sectioned off by color,

I think it's not so much their being
made mostly for men, nor anything in
their being man-made; it's what

they are made *of* disturbs me: rubber
and urethane, plastic aiming for
the plastic of flesh,

and just missing. Growing up, I was
told once that, somewhere in the Vatican,
there's a room still, where—

ordered and numbered, as if
awaiting recall—lie all the phalluses
of stone, granite, tufa, fine marble,

that were removed from pagan statues
for lacking what any leaf, it seems,
can provide: some decorum.

I've never seen them, but their beauty,
I imagine, is twofold: what they're
made of, for one—what, in cracking,

suggests more than just the body that
came first, but the peril,
the vulnerability

that is all the flesh means to say,
singing; then, what even these
imitations before me—lesser somehow

but, to the eye and to touch, finally
more accurate, in being true
to an absurdity that is always there

in the real thing—even these seem
like wanting to tell about beauty,
that it also comes this way, in parts.

Pygmalion

He's up to something, they say.
They say he's had marble carted in
from who knows which of our several
gods knows where. And now he's made
this statue, a woman. The reasons given

for why are as many as we are: that
our women are unclean, and he especially
minds this; that he prefers boys, that
this explains why a statue, that however
much the statue is one of a woman, the

cool marble comes closest to the flesh
that is only a boy's—that hard, and
uncompromising. It is true he has
had some—boys—but what of it?
We are all of us, first and last, human.

If they compare him to the emperor,
the craven Tiberius—Tiberius with his
island of children who romp, lay their
heads, their small open mouths when and
where they're commanded—they're wrong:

the two men are precisely as remote
from each other as history is, always,
from myth. They're wrong, too, when
they say he festoons her, the statue,
with jewels, wants to fuck her. I have

watched him go down to the sea, gather
roses at sunset—it's these that he
offers, and that, later, when he's
lain down beside her, untwines and
removes one by one from her neck.

I have seen him press his flesh to
her marble, hold one of his hands to,
and slowly travel, his own body,
but that's as far as it goes: at that
moment in desire before desire is

finally let go of, when anything could
happen because everything at last is
believed, he leaves off, he says yes to
a sleep like no other. In this respect,
believe all the rest they tell of him:

that he is wisest among us; that he is
truly one who holds the gods' favor.

A Mathematics of Breathing

I

Think of any of several arched
colonnades to a cathedral,

how the arches
like fountains, say,

or certain limits in calculus,
when put to the graph paper's crosstrees,

never quite meet any promised heaven,
instead at their vaulted heights

falling down to the abruptly ending
base of the next column,

smaller, the one smaller
past that, at last

dying, what is
called perspective.

This is the way buildings do it.

II

You have seen them, surely, busy paring
the world down to what it is mostly,

proverb: so many birds in a bush.
Suddenly they take off, and at first

it seems your particular hedge itself
has sighed deeply,

that the birds are what come,
though of course it is just the birds

leaving one space for others.
After they've gone, put your ear to the bush,

listen. There are three sides: the leaves'
releasing of something, your ear where it

finds it, and the air in between, to say
equals. There is maybe a fourth side,

not breathing.

     III
In *One Thousand and One Nights,*
there are only a thousand,

Scheherazade herself is the last one,
for the moment held back,

for a moment all the odds hang even.
The stories she tells she tells mostly

to win another night of watching the prince
drift into a deep sleeping beside her,

the chance to touch one more time
his limbs, going,

gone soft already with dreaming.
When she tells her own story,

Breathe in,
breathe out

is how it starts.

IV

The Man with the Clitoris in His Ear

The man with the clitoris in his ear,
I keep telling myself, means well: if

he's on the phone again, at least this
time he's talking to me, that's something.

Tonight he's tired, he says, but only half
through watching his roommate's copy of

Breakfast at Tiffany's, and he loves it,
he wants to stay up for the end if he can,

he wonders have I seen it, I must have.
But when I say I just finished, minutes

ago, watching my own copy of the very same
movie, he says *spooky,* and then nothing,

just his breathing, sometimes all I think
I need, anymore, of his body, going down,

until the line is too quiet, still as
Kansas from here. I think he thinks I am

lying, or he's thinking what I'm thinking,
fate, fate, like a flag, like a novel.

I think perhaps his silence means only
that the man with the clitoris in his ear

is, at last, asleep now, nothing more.
Whispering into his ear, I say *Careful,*

I say *You could do damage, just dreaming.*

Lullaby for the Wounded Eros

If now, after all that he's
been through, the god lies

Ophelia-fashion, bloodless,
like dying, don't shake him.

If, with his wings and eyes
folded this close to him,

with his half-open mouth at
last making apparent an un-

evenness, what you hadn't
before noticed, to the teeth,

he seems like nothing so
much as any man now, don't

mistake him. Consider how,
for all of the lights out,

his hair shines still, no
different, how his hands,

hidden now where you can't
see them, where his legs

come apart, somehow at the
same time still hold you,

so that even now something
inside stirs: pity,

were it right for any god
to be pitied; fear, maybe;

whatever it is commanding
Be still while you still

can be, Don't wake him.

What Myth Is

Not only what lasts, but what
applies over time also. So
maybe, for all my believing, not

you, on either count. Anymore
than this hand where it falls,
here, on your body; or than

your body itself, however good
sometimes at making—even now,
in sleep—a point carry. Not

this morning, either, that under
the heat has already begun
failing; nor, for all their pre-

Ice Age glamour—what is
mythical, at best, not myth—
these Japanese beetles that off

and on hit the window's limp
screen, fall in, even. Who
make of the trees' leaves a

thin lace the air, like memory,
languidly fingers. Whose wings,
like yours where sometimes I

see them, flash broad, green-
gold in the sun, to say bronze.
When they fold them, it's hard

to believe they fly, ever.

Any Moment

Any moment, you'll rise, wash
yourself down and, without even

noticing all the words that, last
night, while you slept, I whispered

onto your back, come clean.
Meanwhile, as they say, the combination

of doves cooing, or whatever, and
the steady Jamaican rhythm from an

apartment somewhere else, but near,
makes for difficult music. Two wasps

on the rail of the porch look like
fucking, from here. The usual birds,

ascending, like that's where
exultation should be, from one tree

then another, then the one bird,
despite the crowd leaving, not leaving:

the notion that any one of us needs
sometimes to be like him, what's

easier for you to say, maybe. . . .
If you're in the next room, and I

call it another country, the same
thing, is that so strange? The wind

is down, listen. A particular leaf
on its particular branch turns

slightly. A clear morning, so
the edge of the world: everywhere,

how a stranger thing happens.

Étude in D

Late-American. A boy mostly, but with a
man's half-concerns about letting his hair

go, or how his eyes and just under, tired
of waiting him out, show signs of going

without him. Other times—weekends,
the odd stolen day off—any man in boy's

armor: big-boy boots, pants that fail
to hide enough ankle. A name, spelled

backwards, falling somewhere between god
and what's good. All the promise of salt,

how it hangs back on the tongue for a while
after. Connect, miss briefly, try again:

his method. Every word meaning, but the
way something simple—a flower, a bird—

means. A song, but with all the notes left
pending, so a poem. So a kind of music.

Himself the last to give a name to it.

Domestic

If, when studying road atlases
while taking, as you call it, your
morning dump, you shout down to
me names like Miami City, Franconia,
Cancún, as places for you to take
me to from here, can I help it if

all I can think is things that are
stupid, like he loves me he loves me
not? I don't think so. No more
than, some mornings, waking to your
hands around me, and remembering
these are the fingers, the hands I've

over and over given myself to, I can
stop myself from wondering does that
mean they're the same I'll grow
old with. Yesterday, in the café I
keep meaning to show you, I thought
this is how I'll die maybe, alone,

somewhere too far away from wherever
you are then, my heart racing from
espresso and too many cigarettes,
my head down on the table's cool
marble, and the ceiling fan turning
slowly above me, like fortune, the

part of fortune that's half-wished-
for only—it did not seem the worst
way. I thought this is another of
those things I'm always forgetting
to tell you, or don't choose to
tell you, or I tell you but only

in the same way, each morning, I
keep myself from saying too loud I
love you until the moment you flush
the toilet, then I say it, when the
rumble of water running down through
the house could mean anything: flood,

your feet descending the stairs any
moment; any moment the whole world,
all I want of the world, coming down.

The Photographer

Sees with his eyes,

he tells me, like it's the one way,
like there's no room for a question,
there not being out here, where

we're lying, the minimum four sides
required to make a room, no hardwood
floor, no table of deal for any

question to rest on. Is it that
easy? I wonder. Whether, for example,
more and more a circular movement

really does become him, or that more
and more something inside me that
doesn't so much see as feel, mostly,

just thinks so, in the shape his body
finds, sleeping, or in his hand, some
mornings, roughly whisking the day's

eggs. How, from any lawn of birds
rising, he will see the grace only,
me thinking all they prove is how

grace abounding carries only so far,
a different bough, say, a particular
pole over another: who can say

which vision is more true? *There are
whole days,* he tells me, *you see a
thing, you don't see it,* and I want to

A Touring Man Loses His Way

With all the wreckage
of vacation, of an assembled life
in tow, we drive
into this town on
narrowing roads whose names
run verticals up whited stone markers,
suddenly there,
haunting the intersections.

To the right,
in the rush of open vents,
the map crackles idly,
draped and puckering over
her thighs, wide-slung in sleep;
the rich blue interstate prowls
over one knee, and licks
resignedly
the wobbly stick shift.

Above the dust horizon
of dash, and stranded travel-cups,
the sea comes rearing;
then we descend, and the waves

seem to rise from
the quaver of tar and heat
and broken fluorescence.
I say:
"this road,
the road, a
road"
to no one specifically.
Her head wanders from
the headrest, strays
toward the ground sheen of safety glass.

The unamazing thought occurs just
under the wheel-hum
      I have no idea what I am doing
      I have no idea where I am going.
With increasingly waning trust
I grip the wheel—this seems
primary, this feels
correct—and shoulder
by instinct into the hurtling road

that bends, unbends,
buckles through this land: a coast,
shingles flashing, weathering.

Aubade for Eve Under the Arbor

To the buzz and drowse of flies coupling over and over,
I wake, find your body still here, and remember it can
be this way always, us in abundance, visitors few,
behind everything a suggestion of more, ready or not,
where that came from.

                  In those spaces of the world that
the trees, bending aside, give onto, I watch small game
settle and move on, barely long enough for me to assign
them their various names: bush-fowl, blue raven, peahen
with her dull hand of a tail scribbling onto the wet grass
behind her the questions I still can't understand: how
long, when is too much not enough—what price desire?

It is easier for me to believe I came from dirt, having seen
what a little spit and a couple of fingers can do, given
the chance, than that anything torn from my side gave rise
to you, despite evenings when, still awake after turning
from you, I have run my hands up my own body and come
close to saying yes, something's missing. . . . I wonder,

this morning, can you say what it is. I roll over, intending
to ask, but can't wake you, seeing you this quiet, and the sun,
through vines that hold back the sky, throwing shadows, in
thin snakes, across you—look, there is one now, at your ear:
tell me, it seems to say, what can you know of the world?

Levitation

While presumably you
are flying over fields of wild mustard,
deliberate blues and sandstone
that are flax and everything else
flax isn't,

I have spent the days without you
naked and dreaming the traffic
from our bed. The sheets play
Eastern, the right
buttock and elbow rub up against
thin Chinese and blue, outsized
flowers that cannot exist, but
unwind around
and under the body that is always
mine to forget about.

I watch the light in tight cubes raise itself
to powers of brightness
commanding all eyes shut,
and feel the sheets go cinnamon
at my heel (fretting truant, the last
to rise),

then wait for the conquering dream
to come, in which the phone
rings, and knowing
it can only be you, I pass
away from it, into the living room,
my frame shifting over the magazines, litter
of old cups, plates,
and printing the teak-dark floor
with shadow, my body
the one lost cloud.

Imagine my flesh
(leaves waiting to unfurl
in blue sheets)

conquering the dream of you,
as the rooms of my life with you
spin to miniatures below me: the pear
you didn't finish, your votive shoes,
bits I am even now forgetting.

In the Picture

He's younger, early thirties. He's already been
tampered with by the neighbor's maid's daughter

whom his parents, a few times too many, entrusted
him to. Two different men, on separate occasions,

he's taken to Paris; in each case, he's been
disappointed. He has traveled there, once, by

himself, gotten sidetracked, brought a boy back
from Athens, only to find something gives in

translation. He has lost none of his real estate.
He's more trim, works out, doesn't smoke yet,

his hair is differently trained clear of his eyes,
his eyes have fallen but have a way, still, to go.

There are at least two others to come first—
he hasn't met me. At the time of this picture,

I am in an apartment only a few blocks away from
one of his properties, the one the two of us,

eventually, will call home; I am not certain where
I am, except in bed, wondering who's in the shower,

and then remembering; or I am two, maybe three years
into a marriage, and wondering who's in the shower,

and then remembering: the situations are all
equally likely. There are balloons in the picture:

a white one, two reds, a blue, so maybe it's the
fourth of July, or somewhere close to. The balloons

are tied down to the same rail his hand rests on.
They rise, but in the way that balloons, in pictures,

do always: leaden, defiant. He seems happy.

Your Dream

a reinterpretation for Doug

You're wrong.

Not the whitest pigeon
you've ever seen in your life,
but a dove.

The dove not your dead father
come back to remind you
Remember,

the way you insist
he is always there, can't I
see him, every time,

in the busiest parts
of the city, the perfect
space opens to park in.

The dove is your life,
as it has been: absent
of color,

frightened into
a stillness so still
it resembles less

fear than a habit
not minded,
the sofa is warm,

there is somewhere,
not far away,
food. . . .

It is not without meaning
that every one
of the room's windows

is open,
that there are five
windows,

or that the dove,
having flown in by accident
and found himself

trapped,
does not try to escape,
sits seemingly calm

on the sofa,
in a room he suspects
he has, several times over,

been trapped in before.
He is frightened,
but thinking, as hard

as he can,
hard as any bird can.
The one window out

will be ours.

Somewhere Holy

for Erin, for others

There are places in this world where
you can stand somewhere holy and be

thinking If it's holy then why don't
I feel it, something, and while waiting,

like it will any moment happen and
maybe this is it, a man accosts you,

half in his tongue, half in yours, he
asks if maybe you are wanting to get

high, all the time his damaged finger
twitching idly like on purpose at a

leash that holds an animal you can't
quite put your finger on at first, until

you ask him, ask the man, and then
he tells you it's a weasel and, of

course, it is, you've seen them, you
remember now, you say *Of course, a weasel.*

There are men inside the world who, never
mind how much they tell you that they're

trying, can't persuade you that it isn't
you, it's life, it's life in general

where it hurts, a fear, of everything,
of nothing, when if only they would name

it maybe then you'd stay, you all the
time aware it's you that's talking, so

who's going anywhere but here, beside them,
otherwise why come, why keep on coming,

when you can't get to believing what
they tell you any more than you believed

the drugs the other man was offering
wouldn't harm you. Still, you think, you

took them and you're still alive, enough
to take the hand, that wants, that

promises to take you to where damage is
a word, that's all, like yes, so *Yes* you

say, *I'll come,* you tell him *Show me.*

Carl Phillips is the author of one previous volume of poems,
In The Blood, winner of the 1992 Morse Poetry Prize. A recipient
of the Massachusetts Artists Foundation Fellowship and an
Academy of American Poets Prize, he has published widely
in journals including the *Kenyon Review,* the *Paris Review,* and
the *Yale Review,* and in the *Best American Poetry* anthologies
for 1994 and 1995. He is an assistant professor in English
and in African-American Studies at Washington University in
St. Louis, and currently is visiting assistant professor of creative
writing at Harvard University.

Cortège was designed by Will Powers. It is set in the Rotis type family by Stanton Publication Services, Inc., and manufactured by BookCrafters on 55-pound Booktext Natural acid-free paper.